the
AMAZING
Dog Trick Kit

the
AMAZING
Dog Trick Kit

FOR OVERACHIEVING POOCHES
AND THEIR PROUD OWNERS

Steve Duno

CHRONICLE BOOKS

SAN FRANCISCO

Copyright © 2007 becker&mayer!
Illustrations copyright © 2007 Dave Klug

Manufactured in China

Library of Congress Cataloging-In-Publication Data Available

ISBN: 978-0-8118-5850-2

Design: Paul Barrett
Editorial: Meghan Cleary
Production Coordination: Nick Boone-Lutz
Production Development: Peter Schumacher
Project Management: Sheila Kamuda

10 9 8 7 6 5 4 3 2

Chronicle Books LLC
680 Second Street
San Francisco, CA 94107
www.chroniclebooks.com

CONTENTS

INTRODUCTION

Welcome to the wonderful world of dog tricks! Though I'm sure you're already having fun with your dog, that fun is about to increase by leaps and bounds, so get ready. This book contains instructions for 15 tricks and the keys to a closer, more exciting relationship for you and your furry little student.

In addition to providing valuable information about your dog's behaviors, the first part of the book explains how trick training will deepen the bond the two of you already have. Use the included clicker, bell, and flying disc to help teach your pup these show-worthy tricks, and when it's time for a break, use the biscuit cutter to make your pooch some home-made treats! Before you begin, be sure to read the overview carefully, as it provides essential information on how to teach the tricks most effectively.

Are you ready? Great—let the games begin!

OVERVIEW

Though as clever and capable as ever, today's dogs don't have as much to do as their ancestors did. Think of it—for centuries, dogs worked hard guarding property, herding, hunting, driving away rats, and chasing bad guys. They had purpose, and they worked their minds and bodies every day. Being smart, pack-oriented canines, they took to this work naturally.

Like humans, dogs are instinctive learners who crave mental and physical stimulation. Unfortunately, most dogs today get little exercise or mental motivation; many just lie around the house dreaming of chasing squirrels or wondering what's for dinner. The result is that, more often than not, they get bored, listless, and sometimes even fat.

Don't worry—if this sounds like your dog, teaching him tricks is the perfect way to tap into his intelligent canine energy. All dogs have a passion to perform for their owners—it's the combination of their love for us and their breeding for action. Plus, these tricks will give your dog's brain and body a real workout. Regardless of breed, size, or age, you can teach your favorite pal how to put on a great show for all—and most importantly, you'll play your way to owning a very happy dog!

THE BENEFITS
OF TRICK TRAINING

Since your docile doggy is surely cream of the canine crop, it might be hard to believe that your pet is closely related to wild animals. Believe it or not, the social predator mentality of wild wolves has been passed down to your dog, who is as capable of reasoning out complicated behaviors as a cunning wolf or fox. It takes cooperation, communication, and acute brainpower for a wild animal to outthink its prey, and your dog will employ many of these same brain functions in trick training.

Both you and your dog will gain a real sense of accomplishment once you begin training. Because dogs are so smart and adaptable, you may see results immediately. After just a few days of work, you should notice positive improvements in your dog's attitude and awareness. You'll watch as he becomes more enthusiastic and confident, and his attention span will increase as his focus sharpens. Shy dogs will come out of their shells, while bossy dogs will learn to pay closer attention to you.

Many tricks require the dog to actively move his body. Tricks such as *Fetch* or *Catch* can help your dog burn off excess inches gained from lying around the house. You feel better after a good workout, and so will your dog. The extra mental and physical activity will make him happier and more positive, just like these activities do for humans.

Soon, you'll notice a more intimate bond developing between the two of you. That's great! Both of you will look forward to the time spent learning and practicing. What could be better?

BEFORE ENROLLING IN "TRICKS UNIVERSITY"

Before you start, there are some simple guidelines you'll need to know and preparation essentials you'll need to address. If you understand and incorporate these general rules into your training, your dog will learn to respond to your commands quickly—which will make the learning process much more enjoyable. So, to make the most of the experience for both you and your dog, read on!

THE IDEAL TRICK-TRAINING ENVIRONMENT

Begin training in a distraction-free location. That means no other persons, dogs, cats, or rhinos—only you and the dog! It should be a quiet, indoor place, with no threat of interruption at first. Be sure to remove all toys, chews, and food bowls, too.

After your dog can perform a trick in this ideal environment, you should begin introducing minor distractions, one at a time, to perfect the behavior. Make sure to do this for each trick! Ask another person to sit in a nearby chair, then allow the family cat in the room, or turn on the television. Eventually you'll work the trick in the yard, or even at the park. But at first, be sure to perfect the trick in a quiet place!

PATIENCE AND BREVITY

Keep training sessions down to a few minutes, and *always stop while your dog is still interested*. This guarantees he'll be raring to go next time! Also, realize that in the beginning, he may not quite understand what you're trying to teach him; just be very patient, because eventually it'll click. Like people, some dogs learn faster than others, so gauge your dog's learning speed, and be sure not to push him past that. If you move on to a new step too fast and your pup doesn't get it, always move back to the previous step until he nails it. Remember, it's all for your dog's enjoyment!

EQUIPMENT ESSENTIALS

To trick train, you'll need some equipment:

1. A collar with an ID tag is vital, in case your dog runs off when you're working outside. Plus, the collar makes it easy to attach and detach a leash to your pup. Pick whatever style suits your fancy—just be sure it's comfortable and fits snugly so it can't slip off.

2. You'll need a six-foot leash. Leather, cotton, or nylon types work fine, but avoid chain leashes, as they can be harmful to your hands and your dog's face.

3. The clicker, flying disc, and bell included in this kit are all necessary for teaching the tricks in this book.

4. In addition to what comes in the kit, you will also need a few household items: a small amount of masking tape, a small area rug, a balled-up old sock, and a coffee table or cardboard box.

FOOD AND TREATS

The secret to getting your pup to perform is training him just before dinnertime. Why? Because you'll need to use treats to encourage and reinforce the new behaviors. The more responsive your dog is to the treat, the better!

If you let your pet nibble away on food all day (called "free-feeding"), I recommend changing over to scheduled feedings, which will help regulate your dog's appetite, assuring that his food drive will be high during the training session (a side bonus is that it will help prevent obesity).

As your dog begins to master each trick, reduce the frequency of the treat reward, replacing it with simple praise. Instead of giving a treat every time, give one every fifth time. Using treats intermittently at this stage will actually *strengthen* the dog's performance, because it encourages a *heightened expectation*. It's like the excitement of playing a slot machine.

Of course, too many high-calorie treats can make a smart dog fat, so limit treats to pea-size if possible. Avoid using his regular kibble as a treat, because he gets that all the time; instead, try small pieces of cheese, popcorn, chicken, bits of dog cookie, microwaved hotdog slices—anything he really likes.

CLICKER TRAINING
101

Dolphin trainers can't clip a leash to a dolphin. In fact, it's impossible to get a dolphin to do much of anything unless it wants to do it.

So how do dolphin trainers teach their students? It's actually quite simple—they *shape*, or encourage, desirable behaviors with a "marking sound" and a treat. For example, if you want to teach a dolphin to jump out of the water, you wait until the dolphin does it on its own, mark that event with a distinctive sound (like a whistle), and then reward the dolphin with a fish.

It hasn't taken dog trainers long to adapt this training strategy to their own students. Instead of a whistle, they use a metal clicker that makes a distinctive sound when pressed. You own one; try it now.

Here's how it works: When the unusual sound of the clicker is immediately followed by a treat reward, the dog quickly learns that the "click" means something good is coming. The clicker's unique sound "marks" the desired behavior. It's as if you are saying, "Yes, that's exactly what I want you to do!" Paired with a treat, the click becomes an instrument for shaping behavior.

PRIMING YOUR DOG TO THE CLICKER

Before you start trick training, you should teach your dog to associate the "click" with a food reward. Called "priming," this kind of introduction teaches the dog that the click is a wonderful thing.

Priming is easy: Simply click the clicker and *immediately* give him a treat and praise. Do this a dozen times, and repeat the process over the next few days. He'll realize very quickly that the click means good things are coming!

BASIC OBEDIENCE BEHAVIORS

To train the tricks in this book, it will help if your dog knows the basic commands *Sit* and *Down*. Many tricks suggest that you begin with your dog seated or lying down, so it'll be easier for you if you nail these ones right off the bat. Plus, for a dog, these simple behaviors are mental building blocks toward grasping more complicated instructions. If your pup doesn't already know these behaviors, here's how to teach *Sit* and *Down*.

SIT

1. Hold a bit of cheese in your closed hand, then place the hand in front of his nose.

2. Slowly move your hand up and back above his head, keeping it near his sniffing nose, while simultaneously saying "**Rover, sit**" (or whatever his name is!). When you have your hand above his head, he'll look up, causing his back end naturally to drop to a seated position.

3. Immediately say "**good sit!**" in a happy and excited tone. Give him the treat.

Repeat these steps throughout the day. Eventually, you'll use either the upward hand motion or the verbal *Sit* command to get him to sit. After the dog perfects the behavior, reduce treats until you are using them only occasionally. Always praise him for sitting!

DOWN

1. Start with your dog sitting and you crouching in front of him. Hold a bit of cheese in front of his nose.

2. While saying "**Rover, down,**" slowly lower your hand down and away from the dog's nose. He'll follow the cheese down. At this point most dogs will lie all the way down.

3. As soon as he lies down, say "**good down!**" and give him the cheese. Then praise him!

Some dogs will require you to vary the positioning of the treat a bit; experiment with it until you succeed. Think of the treat as a lure. Getting to know what your dog responds to best is part of the fun!

Soon you'll have your dog performing *Down* without treats. Just say "Rover, down!" as you lower your hand in front of him. As with the *Sit* command, you'll eventually be able to use the hand signal or the voice command alone. As your dog gets better at these commands, remember to reduce treats gradually, replacing them with verbal and physical praise.

THE TRICKS

It's time to start training! Remember: Take your time, limit sessions to just a few minutes, and be sure to stop while your dog is still excited to learn. For each trick, make sure you nail each step before proceeding to the next one. Most of all, have fun together and reward your dog with lots of love!

TRICKS TO GET HIS DOGGY NOGGIN GOING

It's a real treat (and quite a feat, too!) to get your dog to communicate with you. These first five tricks will help kick your pup's brain into gear and get you used to the training process. Although these tricks are basic, they may well turn out to be your favorite to perform, since they ask your pup to interact with you in ways that are intelligent, communicative, and downright cute!

1
SHAKE

This one's a real crowd-pleaser and the base from which your pup will learn *Wave* and *Ring the Bell.* Your dog will catch on quickly if you remember always to reward his progress (no matter how slight) with yummy treats!

A HIGH-FIVE FROM FIDO AFTER A HARD DAY'S WORK

1. Crouch before your dog and ask him to *Sit* in front of you atop a nonslip surface, like a carpet. Have treats behind you and your clicker in hand.

2. With your free hand, gently lift one of your dog's feet while simultaneously saying "**Rover, shake.**" As you do, click your clicker, say "**good shake,**" and then reward with a treat. Practice this randomly throughout the first couple of days; eventually your dog will understand that shaking his paw produces a great reward.

3. Next, instead of grabbing his foot, *tap* on the back of his wrist joint with two fingers while saying "**shake**" to coax him into lifting that foot on his own. *Any* movement of the dog's paw, whether initiated by you or by the pup, should be followed by a click, a treat, and happy praise!

4. Gradually reduce the tapping pressure applied to the back of his wrist. The idea is to evoke the foot-lifting response while using less and less pressure, eventually getting the dog to lift his paw simply upon the *anticipation* of you offering your hand.

5. Once the dog voluntarily lifts his paw, begin offering your upturned palm from six to twelve inches away. This becomes the hand signal. You want the dog to respond to the command *without your hand touching him*. Once he does, continue shaping his behavior with the clicker and treats until he responds to the hand signal without a vocal command.

2
WAVE HELLO

Once your pup learns to *Shake*, it's a small step to get him to wave to you. The strategy is to encourage your dog to perform *Shake* from farther and farther away, until the *Shake* becomes in effect a *Wave Hello*. During the training you'll increase your distance and alter the verbal command from "**shake**" to "**wave**," a similar-sounding word. Toward the end you'll again alter it to "**wave hello**," to make the sound more distinctive. In no time, your pooch will *Wave Hello* to you whenever you come home!

A WELL-GROOMED BUTLER WELCOMES GUESTS.

1. With your dog sitting in front of you, ask him to *Shake*. Have him perform *Shake* twice, and click and reward when he does.

2. Now stand up and ask him to *Shake* with your hand a foot away from his paw. If he does it, click, praise, and reward, making sure not to touch his paw. If he won't, go back to a crouching position. Work on this until he'll consistently lift his paw while you are standing with your hand a foot or two away.

3. Slowly change the hand signal from an upturned palm to a fingers-up position, as if you were about to wave. Begin saying "**wave**" instead of "**shake.**"

4. Over time, increase your distance—I'm talking inches at a time. The challenge is to get him to stay in a seated position while you move away.

5. Now begin saying "**wave hello**" instead of "**wave.**" This will help the dog to further distinguish the new trick from *Shake*. You can also teach him to respond only to the hand signal, with no verbal command. Simply give the hand signal, and click and reward any positive response.

3
FIND IT!

This one's easy. Most dogs (especially hungry ones) learn it quickly, as their noses are a hundred times more sensitive than ours. Plus, your pup will love this game of hide-and-go-seek—it'll really get him running around!

A DOMESTICATED HUNT FOR THE PREY DU JOUR

1. With your dog sitting, show him a cookie (hopefully one you baked yourself using a recipe from the back of this book). Then put your hands behind your back and palm the cookie in one hand. In the other, hold your clicker. Bring your fisted hands in front of you and hold them a foot apart, in front of the dog. As you do this, say "find it!" Let the dog sniff both hands; when he sniffs the cookie hand, click, praise, and give him the treat.

2. Practice this several times each day until he gets it. Once he can reliably choose, start varying the type of treat and its size and location. Instead of holding the treat, put it under one of two cups or beneath a bandanna.

3. Once you get your dog to start looking around for hidden treats, you've succeeded in turning on his nose—a potent search engine! Begin hiding treats around the home. Then say "find it!"

4. When he sniffs at the right location, click and reward. Soon you'll be struggling to find a place to hide the treats where he can't find them! (This is the same way police dogs are trained to scent out explosives or drugs!)

4
COOKIE ON NOSE

This trick is sure to amuse your friends and family. The object is to get your dog to balance a cookie on his nose until you give him a release command, causing him to flip the treat up and into his mouth. When done correctly, it's fast and funny! If you have trouble getting him interested, opt for a more desirable treat, such as a square of cheese.

FIDO DISCOVERS THAT PATIENCE IS A VIRTUE.

1. With treats in one pocket and your clicker in hand, crouch in front of your sitting or standing dog. With your free hand, hold the end of his muzzle steady for a second, then click and reward. Work on increasing the time you hold his muzzle, clicking when he reaches that time limit. Then praise and reward with a treat.

2. The next time you hold his muzzle, place a cookie on it, closer to his nose than to his eyes. Say "**wait**," then slowly let go of his muzzle and wait a second or two. Then click, praise, and give him the cookie. If he tries to flick the cookie off and mow through it, don't scold him, but also don't give any rewards.

3. Place the cookie on his nose and say "**wait**." After ten seconds, happily say "**okay!**" The first few times you try this he'll probably wait a second, then drop the cookie. Don't click or reward; simply replace the cookie and try again. When he gets lucky and catches it in his mouth, click, reward, and praise mightily!

5

RING THE BELL

How would you like it if your doggy could say "I have to go to the bathroom. Could you please open the door for me?" Well, this trick won't exactly teach him that, but *almost*! Once your dog masters it, he *will* be able to ask politely to go outside to relieve himself! The goal is to have your pooch *Ring the Bell* whenever nature calls. You'll have it tied to the appropriate doorknob (at your dog's shoulder height); he'll walk up and jingle it with his paw or nose.

A DIGNIFIED PLEA FOR A BATHROOM BREAK

1. First you'll teach your dog to associate the sound of the bell with going outside. Hang the bell from the doorknob. Choose a door without accessible glass, unless it's thick safety glass. Using a leash, bring him to the hanging bell, then jingle it yourself while excitedly saying "**outside!**" Then, open the door and enthusiastically take him to the potty zone.

2. Next, bring him to the bell and ask him to *Shake* (which you hopefully have already taught him). Position him so that the path of his paw lifts into the bell. Place your offered hand close to the bell to increase the odds of him hitting it. If his paw touches the bell *at all*, click, reward, and praise! Immediately say "**outside!**" and take him out.

3. Next, slowly phase out the verbal *Shake* command, and only offer your hand. Position the dog so his paw will strike the bell. Click and reward whenever he rings it, then take him outside.

4. Eventually, instead of offering your hand, point to the bell and happily say "**outside!**" This is a key step, as you are bridging behaviors. Instead of thinking he's shaking hands, he must now understand that he is pawing the bell. Be patient!

5. Now, with his leash on, lead your dog to the bell, point to it, and say "**outside!**" Ideally, he should paw at the bell. If he rings the bell with his muzzle instead of his paw, that's fine!

6. The last step is to take him to the door without saying or doing anything. Try this after dinner, when he'll need to potty. If he bats the bell, click, reward with a special treat, and then take him out and bow down to your stellar student!

HEY!

COME WATCH WHAT MY DOG CAN DO!

Now that your pup's responding to your commands, let's start to work off some of those treats! The next five tricks will test your budding skills at trick training—and they're designed to give your pup an extra challenge, too.

6
SPEAK!

Speak adds your dog's voice to the training sessions. It differs from other behaviors in that you can't *make* your dog vocalize; instead you have either to wait for him to bark or find a stimulus trigger that incites him to bark. Once he barks, mark and shape the behavior with the clicker, cookies, and praise.

FIDO RESPECTFULLY REQUESTS A HAMBONE.

1. Find a situation that makes your dog bark. Does he bark at the doorbell or at a knock at the door? If the doorbell or knock won't squeeze a bark from his lips, try active play, blowing in his face, or barking at him! Even a stranger or dog walking by might work; you just have to find that trigger.

2. If he barks at a knock or a ring, have your dog sit in front of you, then get a friend to knock or ring the doorbell. Simultaneously give a unique hand signal with your free hand; I use a closed fist "knocking" the air. (Use the hand signal *before* the verbal command, so the dog doesn't get confused listening to your voice and the sound of the stimulus at the same time.)

3. If your dog barks, immediately click, reward, and praise. Any vocalization at this point is good. By now he understands that hearing the click means "that's right!"

4. Once he begins barking on the hand signal, phase out the initial trigger and replace it with the verbal command "**speak!**" Say it simultaneously with the hand signal, and click when he barks. Between attempts, play with him to keep him in an excited state that will encourage barking. Eventually, you can phase out the clicker and treats, and your pup will not only wave hello, but *say* hello when you get home!

7
SPIN

The challenge of teaching *Spin* lies in your ability to bait your dog into moving in a fast, tight circle. The key is learning how to gradually reduce the role your hand plays. It'll take practice, but you'll get it! Make sure your pooch is plenty hungry. And consider using *really* delectable treats, like bits of chicken or cheese.

FIDO UNWINDS COUNTERCLOCKWISE THE SECOND TIME AROUND.

1. With your dog standing in front of you, show him the treat. Then hold the tidbit an inch from his nose and repeatedly say "**spin**," while patiently baiting him around in a full circle. Experiment with the positioning of your baiting hand, and don't let him swipe the treat from you! Remember, you are shaping behavior, so even a partial response right now is good.

2. Work this until he'll spin full circle when lured by the treat. Then try luring him faster, so that eventually he'll spin quickly. Also, tighten up the spin so that he's pivoting rather than circling.

3. Next, instead of luring the dog with the treat held in front of his nose, try holding your treat hand above the dog's head while making the circular motion. The idea is to change your hand movement gradually from a baiting motion (that he follows) to a tight circular sign above him. This becomes the hand signal for *Spin*.

4. Now, without a treat in hand, make a small circular motion with your finger while saying "**spin!**" once. You've done it—now make sure to practice both directions so your pup can unwind!

8

WIPE YOUR FACE

Ready for a challenge? Some dogs learn this trick in a day, but others take weeks. Let's see how your furball does! Clicker timing is *crucial* with this trick.

CLEANLINESS IS NEXT TO DOGLINESS.

1. Ask your dog to *Sit* in front of you, and place an inch-long piece of masking tape *loosely* onto his right eyebrow. Get your clicker ready, as many dogs will immediately paw the tape off.

2. After placing the tape, say "**wipe your face**" while simultaneously giving the hand signal, a quick wipe of your own brow. Click, reward, and praise *the instant* the dog wipes its face.

3. Next, move the tape up onto his forehead, so that you can eventually get him to wipe his paw from the top of his head all the way down past his muzzle. Once he regularly wipes the tape off, reduce its size, so that after a week he'll wipe off even a tiny dot of tape.

4. Eventually you'll eliminate the tape and gradually increase your distance from the dog, while phasing out the clicker in favor of the verbal command.

9
TAKE A BOW

You've seen it when he stretches in the morning, or when he gets down into that playful "catch me" posture. The trick to teaching *Take a Bow* is to get him to assume that position when asked. This may take a while, so be sure to click and reward *any* positive attempts. When you get your dog to *Bow* without helping him, you've really accomplished something! If you both have made it this far already, he sure deserves to take a bow!

A GENTEEL PERFORMANCE IN EXCHANGE FOR PRAISE

1. One way to teach this trick is to keep your clicker and treats on hand, in case the dog assumes the *Bow* position on his own. If you click and reward the behavior the *second* it occurs (like during his morning stretch), you'll have success.

2. Slip in a hand signal when he bows on his own; I use a right-sweeping, downward motion of my right hand (as if tossing dice onto the floor), to differentiate it from the vertically falling *Down* hand signal. Say "**good bow!**"

3. If he doesn't bow on his own, don't fret. Have him stand while you crouch down on his right. Slip your left knee or left hand loosely beneath his tummy, close to his hind legs. Place a treat below his head on the floor, then sign and say "**down**" while gently keeping his tummy elevated.

4. He'll be confused, so be patient. If necessary, gently lower his front end with pressure on his shoulders. When he gets close to the *Bow* position, click and reward, then phase out the extra nudges!

5. Next, with him standing and you crouched just left of his head, place a treat on the floor below his head and say "**bow**." Use "bow" instead of "down," to bridge from a known behavior to a new one with a similar-sounding word.

6. Use the sweeping *Bow* hand signal instead of the one for *Down*. If his back end starts dropping, touch him on the belly to prevent it from lowering.

7. Again, change the verbal command slightly to further differentiate from the "down" sound. Now both of you—*Take a Bow!*

10

GO TO THE RUG

When your pup is underfoot, there's nothing better than being able to ask him to go sit quietly on his rug. Guests will be quite impressed when you say "**go to the rug**," and the pup trots over to his rug and patiently waits there.

A POOCH WINS POINTS FOR ENDURANCE.

1. Place a small, nonslip rug in a quiet area. Clip on Rover's leash and, while he's watching, drop a treat onto the rug. Walk around with him, then happily trot him over to the rug while saying "**go to the rug!**" When he steps onto the rug (and before he inhales the treat), click, and praise!

2. Next, instead of leading him all the way to the rug, let go of the leash when three feet away, then five feet, then ten, etc. You'll gradually get him to go to the rug on his own to get the treat. Click and praise only when he steps completely onto the rug, with all feet on it. Work on this until you can let go of the leash from across the room and have him frolic over to the rug all by himself at your command.

3. Now teach him to wait on the rug. Place a treat on the rug, say "**go to the rug**," then lead him over on the leash. Click and praise, then say "**wait.**" Give a hand signal to make him wait—I use a sideways palm like a stop sign pushed in his direction.

4. Back off a few feet while repeating "**wait**" and giving the hand signal. Have him wait ten seconds, then happily say "**okay!**"

5. Increase the amount of time he'll wait on the rug. To shape this, delay the click and reward for a longer period each time. Eventually he'll be able to *Go to the Rug* and wait there for thirty minutes! He can stand, sit, lie down, or sleep—it doesn't matter so long as he doesn't leave the rug.

SUPER-AMAZING,
UTTERLY STUPENDOUS TRICKS!

Congratulations—you and your whiz kid are at the head of the class! The following five tricks are for the well-seasoned trickster; they ask your pup to confidently show off for your guests. What a ham!

11
WALK BACKWARD

It's quite a sight to see a dog walk backward (outside of the circus)! The setup for this trick is key. You must create a training venue that limits your dog's side-to-side movement, only allowing backward-forward motion. I use the narrow space between a sofa and a coffee table; you can try this, or set up a narrow alleyway between a wall and a sofa or some other long object. Make the training alley only a foot or so wider than the dog and at least five feet in length.

FIDO DOES THE MOONWALK.

1. Have your dog stand near the front of the training alley. With treat and clicker in hand, walk toward him briskly while saying "**back up**." Use a hand signal simultaneously; try moving both hands away from your body in a quick pushing motion.

2. Experiment with your posture and speed. Often a dog will actually need the trainer to walk right into him before moving backward. If he sits, just happily put him back into a standing position and try again. Sometimes, shuffling your feet while moving toward the dog helps. Be upbeat and positive, as your initial move forward might worry some dogs.

3. Next, try the trick without the alleyway, in the middle of a quiet, carpeted room. Don't back the dog up into a wall, door, or window! If he forgets how to back up, go back to using the alleyway.

4. Now encourage him to back up without you using your body as the trigger. Start the trick as usual, but take only a step or two toward him. Then reduce the distance you need to advance until you can initiate the behavior from a standing position using just the verbal command and hand signal. This is the key step! Hold off on the click and reward until he can *Walk Backward* a good six feet.

12
CRAWL COMMANDO

This neat trick will get your dog crawling like a foot soldier deep in the brush. As with all acquired abilities, this movement may take a while to sink into your pup's brain but will certainly be a crowd-pleaser when it does! To teach your pooch to crawl, you'll need to set up a training situation that initially inhibits him from standing. I've had luck using a coffee table. What you use will depend upon the size of your dog and what you have available. You might use a 3-by-6-foot section of cardboard or plywood atop piles of books, or even a cardboard box with both ends open. Also, make sure that Rover is very hungry, so he'll do almost *anything* for that treat!

FIDO POSES AS A GUARD DOG.

1. With the dog in a *Down* position on the long side of a coffee table (or whatever device you decide to use), get down low on the opposite side. Say "**Rover, crawl**," then bait him toward you with a treat (use chicken or cheese). He'll have to crawl across the short distance beneath the coffee table to get at it. Use a unique hand signal; I waggle my hand back and forth quickly while holding the treat in my fingers, as if turning a screwdriver.

2. Make sure the treat is held close enough to entice him. Move the treat slowly enough to keep his attention, but fast enough to keep him moving. Be sure to click and reward before he stands up!

3. Now try having him crawl *lengthwise* beneath the table or confinement. He might have to crawl at least three times as far, so be patient.

4. Now take off the training wheels. With the dog in a *Down* position on the carpet, try the same procedure, only *without* the coffee table or confinement apparatus.

5. Once you perfect the *Crawl Commando* in the quiet space, try it in different areas of the home, and outdoors too. In no time, your dog will be creeping around your home with the intensity of a commando!

13
CATCH!

Here's a trick that's been taught to dogs for centuries. Now it's your pooch's turn to play ball! However, catching things isn't an instinctive behavior for a dog, so you'll have to break him in slowly and without distractions.

A PROFESSIONAL MAKES IT LOOK EASY.

1. First, get some popcorn. Ask him to *Sit*, and let him sniff the treat. Holding one piece about a foot above his head, say "**catch!**" and then drop it into his mouth before he jumps up. If he catches it, click, and give him another piece as a reward.

2. Next, ask him to *Sit*, then say "**catch!**" and toss a piece at him from two feet away. Keep working until he can catch the thrown popcorn.

3. Now switch to a cookie, which can be thrown farther than a piece of popcorn. Start from a few feet away and gradually increase the distance. Cookies travel faster, so take it easy. Click and reward only if he catches it.

4. Once he can catch a cookie from ten feet away, change to a balled-up sock with a treat inside. Consider making the reward treat different from the thrown cookie—perhaps chicken or cheese. Say "**catch**," throw it to him from a few feet away, and click and reward when he catches it. Since you don't want him to eat the sock, when you're working a sock or ball *Catch* from a distance, excitedly call him over after clicking, take the object, and *then* give him his reward.

5. Move on to a tennis ball (or something smaller for tiny dogs—many pet stores carry 2- and 3-inch Nerf balls that work well). Start out close, and consider smearing a dot of peanut butter onto the ball. Always give the verbal command. Click if he catches it, then call him over for the reward. Increase your distance until he'll catch it from ten feet away.

6. Now go outside. Start close to your dog, and increase distance until he can *Catch* from across the yard. Reduce treats, phase out the clicker, then sign him up for Little League!

14

FLYING DISC FETCH

Canine disc competitions happen all over the world, so get your pooch started on this great organized activity! Before starting to train, acquaint your dog with the flying disc. Turn the toy upside down and feed him from it for a week. Later, when he sees his food dish floating through the air, he'll definitely want to go after it!

LOCAL DOG CATCHES FLYING SAUCER.

1. Sit on the floor with your dog in a quiet room and play with the disc. Tease him with it, then offer it to him. It helps to have a dab of peanut butter on it initially. Roll the disc from hand to hand. Play "keep-away" with him. Make the disc seem like the cat's meow.

2. Now, with clicker and treats at hand, roll the disc at him and say "**catch!**" If he grabs it, click, reward, and praise. Work on this for a minute, then stop while he is still excited.

3. Next, try rolling the disc down a hallway, then saying "**fetch!**" If he chases it, click and praise, then happily say "**here!**" while displaying a treat. At this stage you are bridging from "catch" to "fetch." When you say "**here**," get low and be happy!

4. Once he'll chase the rolling disc and bring it back, try tossing it to him from a few feet away. If he catches it, click, praise, then call him. Take the disc and give him a treat. Work this until he can reliably catch it and bring it over. Remember—short, fun sessions!

5. Now to the heart of it: In a large room or garage, have the dog sit beside you. Show him the disc (with some peanut butter on it), tease him a bit, then toss it up and out, just a foot or two above and in front of him. (Try to loft it up so that he can easily catch it; you'll have to experiment with the right positioning and techniques.) Simultaneously say "**fetch!**" If you're

lucky, he'll jump out and catch it. If he does, click, praise, get down low with a treat, then excitedly say "**here!**" When he comes over with the disc, celebrate!

6. Now move to a quiet fenced yard or tennis court. Loft it up close, and click if he catches it. Lengthen the distance, and be sure to toss the disc in just the right way. If he catches it and runs off, you may need to attach a retractable lead or length of rope to him to guarantee that he'll return each time. The *Flying Disc Fetch* won't mean much unless he returns!

7. If you trust your dog to come back reliably when called, move to the park. Start with short throws and use any available breezes to keep the disc hovering. Toss it into the wind to improve his chances of grabbing it. Be sure to get down low, happily call him over, and remember to have short sessions that end while his motor is still happily humming!

8. If you want to advance even further, purchase a full-size, dog-friendly throwing disc; they fly farther, higher, and slower. You might even check out local canine disc competitions. Who knows? He could even bring home a trophy!

15

ACHOO!

If your dog can learn this one, he'll earn his keep whenever you catch a cold. The goal is to get your pup to walk over to a tissue box, pull out a tissue, and bring it to you whenever you sneeze. Whether or not you choose to *use* the thing, this is a neat parlor trick that your guests will surely love!

A FUZZY-MUZZLED NURSE DELIVERS TISSUES.

1. With your dog beside you and a box of tissues at hand, loosen a tissue so it's flagging way up out of the box. Tease him by waving the box and flagging tissue under his nose. Let the tissue tickle him; keep at it until he tries to grab it. While teasing him, keep repeating "**achoo!**" Eventually he'll grab the tissue; when he does, click, reward, and praise!

2. Begin pulling the tissue up out of the box less and less, until he'll grab it with only the normal amount flagging up. This may take days of patient work, so hang in there!

3. Now place the box atop a platform the dog can easily reach. Flag the tissue way out of the box, and repeat "**achoo!**" If necessary, teasingly move the box around until he'll grab the tissue. Eventually you want him to pull a tissue from the stationary box without being teased. (Note: Tape the box down to steady it.)

4. *Gradually* increase your distance from the box. At some point your pup will need to learn that once he has the tissue, he needs to bring it over to you. When he has it, excitedly call him over as you would for *Fetch*. Delay the click and reward until he brings it over and lets you take it.

5. Increase his starting distance from the box. Give the command when he's a foot away, then two, then three, until after a week or so, he's across the room. For this phase you should sit beside the platform holding the box. This will increase the odds that he'll walk over.

6. Begin placing the box farther from yourself. While he sits waiting six feet from the box, take a seat far away from the box. Then say "**achoo!**" a few times. If you've trained patiently, he'll go to the box and grab a tissue. If necessary, praise while he's trying, but don't click until he brings it over. Feel free to return to an earlier stage if he gets confused.

HOME COOKING
FOR FIDO

By now, your expert trickster deserves top-of-the-line rewards! Here are two great recipes for baking home-made snacks he'll love. Be sure to use the bone-shaped cookie cutter provided in the kit.

HOMEMADE DOG COOKIES

INGREDIENTS:

- 3 cups whole-wheat flour
- 1 cup oatmeal
- 1/4 cup powdered milk
- 1 cup chicken or beef stock
- 1/2 teaspoon olive oil
- 1/2 cup vegetable shortening
- 2 eggs
- 1/4 cup shredded Cheddar cheese

First, get the dog out of the kitchen (have him *Go to the Rug*). Preheat the oven to 350° F. Next, mix all ingredients together in a large bowl. Fine-tune flour or liquid as needed to create a firm dough with the consistency of modeling clay. Knead well, then roll out into a 3/8-inch sheet, dusting with flour if necessary. Be sure not to roll the dough any thicker than 3/8-inch, as this will increase cooking time substantially. Then, using your bone-shaped cookie cutter, punch out cookies and place them on an ungreased nonstick cookie sheet. Bake for thirty minutes, or until crisp and brown. Be sure to cool before serving. Using the bone-shaped cookie cutter, this recipe makes approximately twenty cookies. Stored in a plastic bag in the refrigerator, they should keep for two weeks. And remember, *they're for the dog.*

PEANUT-BUTTER BISCUITS

INGREDIENTS:

- 2 cups whole-wheat flour
- 1 tablespoon baking powder
- $1/4$ teaspoon garlic powder
- $1/2$ cup smooth peanut butter
- 1 egg
- 1 cup whole milk
- $1/4$ cup vegetable shortening

Send the dog to the neighbor's. Preheat the oven to 375° F. Then, in a large bowl, mix dry ingredients and set aside. In a blender, mix peanut butter, egg, and milk together until smooth. Now fold peanut butter mixture into the dry ingredients. Add shortening and adjust flour and liquid as needed to make a firm, workable dough. After kneading, roll out into a $3/8$-inch-thick sheet, dusting with flour if necessary. Punch out cookies with the included cookie cutter and place on an ungreased, nonstick baking sheet. Bake for twenty minutes, or until crisp and brown. Makes approximately twenty cookies, which will stay fresh for two weeks in a plastic bag in the refrigerator. Cool before serving, and don't let your kids get to them first!

CONCLUSION

So you've become a crackerjack dog trainer and taught your pooch some cool tricks. Good job! You've strengthened the bond between you and learned how to speak your dog's language. Nothing feels better than having your dog look at you with an excited, confident look that says, "Come on, let's learn something new!"

Be sure to keep working on the tricks with your dog, fine-tuning his performance and quickening his reaction time. But don't stop there: Consider designing and teaching your own tricks, or even training the neighbor's dog. Take your dog to obedience, agility, tracking, herding, or "flyball" classes, or enter a flying disc tournament. Read more books on dog behavior and go to a dog park, where your pup can have unlimited fun with his furry friends. There are a whole host of activities you and your dog can participate in together—this book of tricks may have been your first experience, but don't let it be your last!

ACKNOWLEDGMENTS

I'd like to thank all at becker&mayer! for their help with this book, especially Meghan Cleary and Paul Barrett, as well as Dave Klug. Their excellent editorial, design, and artistic skills have made the entire experience as relaxed and enjoyable as possible. Thanks also to Chronicle Books for embracing the idea that trick training for dogs can be fun and exciting for everyone, including humans!

ABOUT THE AUTHOR

Veteran pet behaviorist and author **Steve Duno** has written thirteen books, as well as many magazine and Web articles. He has covered a wide variety of subjects, including basic training, tricks, aggression, behavior modification, breed profiling, and pet health care.

Formerly a teacher in New York City and Los Angeles, Steve has had numerous appearances on Seattle news stations KOMO and King-5, as well as frequent stints on local and national radio. He currently lives in Seattle with his family and an ever-changing assortment of rescued pets.